TRADING WITH THE A-LINE

HOW ANYONE CAN MAKE MONEY IN THE STOCK MARKET

Aberdeen Trading

ABOUT IAN ABERDEEN

After Ian Aberdeen graduated from Melbourne University he managed his family business and then operated a business consultancy for the next for 45 years, one of the highlights of which, during the reign of President Marcos, involved overseeing some of the large scale Philippine economic infrastructure projects for the World Bank. He has traded shares and operated a family superannuation fund for the last 30 years, and is a long-standing member of the Australian Technical Analysts Association. Over the last 10 years he has developed some simple share-trading tools which generate daily reports on trading results and identifies shares to sell. Prior to the Global Financial Crisis (GFC) hitting home he nervously sold his entire portfolio based on *The A-Line Trading Strategy*. That decision proved to be one of the best moves of his trading career.

ABOUT IAIN MCLEAN

Iain McLean holds degrees in Structural Engineering and Psychology and a HND in Construction Management: Structural Mechanics & Contract Law. He has been involved in management roles for the last 15 years. Iain has worked in the UK, the USA and Australia as an engineer, director and owner with various businesses and is a current member of the Australian Technical Analysts Association. He also consults with Small to Medium Enterprises to help them improve productivity and process efficacy.

TRADING WITH THE A-LINE

How anyone can make money in the stock market

Ian Aberdeen

&

Iain McLean

Published by The Countryside Academy Pty Ltd 2014

www.aberdeenstockmarkettrading.com

Copyright © 2014 The Countryside Academy Pty Ltd

This publication is copyright. All rights reserved. Except as permitted under the Copyright Act 1968, no part of this publication may be reproduced, stored or transmitted by any means, electronic or otherwise, without the specific written permission of the copyright owner.

Aberdeen Trading is a registered trading name of The Countryside Academy Pty Ltd

First Printing: 2014

ISBN 978-1-326-04238-7

The Countryside Academy
PO Box 4099, 631 Glen Huntley Road
Hopetoun Gardens, VIC 3162

Ordering Information:
Special discounts are available on quantity purchases by corporations, associations, educators, and others. For details, contact the publisher at the above listed address.

CONTENTS

About Ian Aberdeen ii
About Iain McLean ii
Who Should read this book? vii
Our disclaimer ix
The purpose of this book xi
An introduction to the A-Line 13
The A-Line difference 14
A universal problem 15
A managed fund or self-managed money? 17
Why small funds have an edge 20
Using our tools is easy 21
    Our mantra: 21
The A-Line trading strategy 22
Capital needed to start trading shares 24
The share trading process 25
Trialing the A-Line strategy 26
In conclusion 27
Appendices 29
Calculating compound interest 31
Self-managed small share funds have an edge 33
Thank you! 35
Notes 37

WHO SHOULD READ THIS BOOK?

This book is for anyone in Australia who is of working age, approaching retirement or already retired.

This book is for anyone looking to increase their financial wealth and improve their lifestyle.

This book is for anyone who has the aptitude to set aside 30 minutes each weekday and follow a defined set of simple rules.

OUR DISCLAIMER

We are not registered financial advisers. We do not solicit or seek to know your individual financial arrangements. We will not recommend share trading as the best option in your circumstances, nor will we advise any particular share or shares which you should buy or sell. In addition to receiving this letter you should be consulting your accountant, your solicitor and your financial advisor before you start share trading. In each newsletter we only supply data and trading tactics for you as the financial manager to use.

Even if you do not follow instructions from a registered financial advisor, it is important that you find an accountant who deals with superannuation accounts, and a solicitor known to your accountant, so that your management of your family investment funds is both legal and based on business entities which minimise the taxes you pay.

Share trading carries risks, but if carefully managed using our tools we find that it can deliver results which improve your finances in retirement to a comfortable level. You are managing your finances and you will be the one to make a series of decisions if you commit to following this system.

In the series of chapters that follow we describe the steps you need to take to start trading, make a profit and avoid any serious loss.

THE PURPOSE OF THIS BOOK

This introduction to Aberdeen Trading, our trading strategy and our unique, proprietary market indicator The A-LINE is to allow you, the interested party to do your due diligence and evaluate for yourself our offering before committing your money to joining the other already successful subscribers to our weekly newsletter.

Above all else we advocate risk management. You must consider your own situation in isolation and in conjunction with being a member of The A-Line subscriber community to determine if it is the right and proper choice for you.

In the following pages of this free document we will set out the basics of personal finance management, the current economic climate here in Australia and how trading with The A-Line by subscribing to our newsletter can allow you to use the capital you already possess and increase it with managed risk and astute technical analysis.

When you subscribe to our The A-Line Newsletter you will be joining the already happy members of a successful trading community. We will teach you how to implement the tools we provide, introduce you to market psychometrics and price valuations and how they can be examined with relative ease using our trading strategy.

AN INTRODUCTION TO THE A-LINE

The A-Line is a proprietary indicator and intellectual property owned and developed solely by Aberdeen Trading to minimize financial risk during trading. We have been trading our own personal portfolios by using the A-Line as our primary indicator since its inception. If your Introduction requires multiple pages, the final page should be on an even numbered page (left side of an open book). A section break is included below to automatically insert the required blank page if required.

When the Global Financial Crisis struck in 2009 we were already developing the A-Line as an indicator of the Australian share market to reduce risk. The power of the A-Line prevented the GFC from negatively impacting our capital. As we followed our own A-Line Trading Strategy we watched as reports hit the financial pages of traders and investors losing all their capital as they clung to the hope that the GFC was only a minor hiccup.

Unimpressed by most of the media share reporting and advice available we have decided to share our A-Line Trading Strategy with the thousands of Australians managing investment funds via a subscription based newsletter.

Each newsletter will be emailed to recipients weekly and will take only two minutes to read but will report on both market trends and moods.

Each newsletter will teach you how to use a simple trading tool and will list three new shares worth considering using evidence-based share trading.

THE A-LINE DIFFERENCE

What the A-Line measures is market mood but not in the same way as the VIX

The Chicago Board Options Volatility Index (The VIX) measures the implied volatility of S&P 500 index options. Traders frequently call the VIX the fear index. When the VIX rises, caution is to be exercised. The VIX is calculated and distributed in real-time by The Chicago Board Options Exchange and is calculated by using current market prices for all out-of-the-money calls and puts for the front month and second month expirations.

Stepping back a moment and covering some basics on price it must be understood that price is simply a record of the level of financial value a person places on a product. Using simple supply and demand curves, if demand outstrips supply price increases and vice versa as buyers place more value on product as it becomes scarcer.

We can use multiple measures of price to show what the markets are doing but the most powerful extraneous variable in trading is the human element. Human emotions have both positive and negative impacts on trading every day. In an effort to isolate this emotion and apply a metric to it so the powerful variable of emotion can be standardized in a statistical format and used to lower risk in the decision making process of trading we at Aberdeen Trading developed the A-Line.

The A-Line is a psychometric measure of market mood in which error variables associated with price fluctuation are removed to increase the A-Line's statistical validity and power.

A UNIVERSAL PROBLEM

If you are interested in growing your wealth, particularly to fund your retirement, consider trading using our A-Line strategy

An ageing population, a smaller percentage of workers to support those who are either too young or too old to work and an increasing chasm between the ordinary person in the street and the rich are all symptoms of how improved healthcare and social-wellbeing have impacted us. You cannot have the positive without the negative. This is a key to what we will share with you. Life is about taking risks but those people who are successful are those who carefully work to a rigid strategy of risk management. That is what we at Aberdeen Trading have spent the last few years designing; simple and effective tools to minimise risk and give traders a previously unavailable edge with which to grown their wealth.

At school you are taught the basics or reading, writing and arithmetic. Depending on how far you go in high school or university you can study some very complex subjects but no matter if you end up working as a tradie or surgeon there's one thing that binds us all and that is money; how it's made how we make it, how we use it and how we lose it. It's also the one subject that isn't taught in school so most people leave school not knowing much about the single most impacting facet of their lives: money management.

That leaves the door open to debt and financial problems. When you get in debt it's a hard downward spiral to break. The rich won't share their wealth. Why should they? They no doubt worked very hard for it. If you want to live a lifestyle that allows you to enjoy your family, friends and everything that you are involved in you need to begin preparing the foundations for financial freedom. The figures that are freely available to anyone via the Australian Bureau of Statistics clearly show that an increasing number of the population will end up on a shrinking old-age pension. That statement may scare you. If it does, and you consider yourself to be in that group, then we can help you.

Don't worry if you didn't get a master's degree in applied economics or if you started on the back-foot financially or were unable to earn money through a full working life for whatever reason. A vast majority of Australians are facing the fact that they may never be able to build a Super Fund or other retirement investment that will be sufficient to see them through their retirement. There are two common methods to change this, namely buying investment property or trading on the stock market.

We advocate trading on the stock market because the barriers to entry are much lower and the financial risks involved can be reduced to have a far lesser effect on your finances than any property investment ever could. Consider a market down-turn at a time when you need access to your invested finances. If you have invested in property you may never recoup your losses from the downturn whereas by using a suitable trading strategy you can liquidate investments almost instantly using internet trade accounts and keep your money safe as the market continues to tumble.

The trick in share trading is not making a profit but not losing that profit, so that over time the compounding interest effect will grow your fund. There are well known strategies and tactics for greatly reducing any losses and building your profits. We trade shares using those methods, and have developed simple tools to keep you focused on the bottom line.

A MANAGED FUND OR SELF-MANAGED MONEY?

To begin to self-manage your savings or super fund via trading you have two basic options:

- Invest your money in a managed fund, sit back and hope you get the return on investment you wanted
or
- Manage the growth of your own finances, taking only the risks you deem appropriate for your money after considering your situation and the target return on a particular investment.

The current Federal Government and their implementation of Hockeynomics demonstrate that we all have to look out for ourselves in a fragmented and sectarian society as the Federal Government, under Prime Minister Tony Abbot, moves to restrict and block handouts and subsidies to both private individuals and industry.

While over-indulgence into handouts and subsidies can lead to reliance and the possibility of financial atrophy, similarly the carte blanche cessation of such socioeconomic infrastructure tools in general can have equally negative effects on the population in general and their financial well-being.

To remedy both, we at Aberdeen Trading suggest a simple system of checks and balances to allow the individual to maximize their financial position in respect of their individual situation, allowing greater freedom and choice.

One method to leverage your savings and maximize your earnings that is freely available to anyone is to build your superannuation account. This can be either in a managed fund or in a Self-Managed Super fund.

Sadly, most high school and tertiary education courses fail to teach what is arguably the one of the most prevalent causes of stress and associated ill-health; financial management.

By following the guidelines and rules in trading systems such as that offered by Aberdeen Trading you will be educating yourself as to how you can use the resources available to you in new and possibly previously unconsidered ways to reduce your debt and increase your assets, allowing you an increased net wealth and the freedom of choice that come with such an improvement in lifestyle.

As we stated at the beginning of this document, you cannot expect to reap the benefits without some negative elements but by applying an appropriate methodology the negative aspects can mediated or factored out of the equation.

What follows is a simple list of the pros and cons of trading using our A-Line Trading Strategy:

Potential benefits that can expect are:

- You avoid paying a management fee (see the appendix for more information).
- By trading shares through an internet broker your buying and selling costs are dramatically reduced than if you trade through a conventional bricks-and-mortar brokerage firm.
- Small traders can use their limitations to their advantage by researching and buying stocks in small cap and technology companies which are typically too volatile for large institutional investment firms (see the article in the appendix for more information).
- Managing your own fund puts routine into your retirement lifestyle, a proven psychological benefit that leads to increased personal well-being.
- If you manage your funds well you can pass on the knowledge and skills you have learned to your children

and grandchildren to allow them to secure their own financial freedom.

Potential problems you may face are:

- You must adhere strictly to a few well-known and well-documented rules of share trading for profit, which we will explain to new subscribers. Not everyone is capable of following these rules.
- Some computer programs for charting and trading shares are complicated and some users never fully learn how to use all the features correctly.

Our Risk Management

As part of our risk management ideology we will point you in the direction of simple to use, yet effective charting and trading programs which we know how to use.

We will also provide new subscribers with a set of simple trading tools that will facilitate your daily trading chores and quickly confront you with any problems that may arise.

WHY SMALL FUNDS HAVE AN EDGE

There is a world of difference between managing share-trading in a multi-million dollar investment fund and self-managing your own small fund. The large fund deals mostly or exclusively with blue chip shares that own large amounts of capital (large-cap) and are included in the ASX300 group. It is not uncommon to see a share price jump once it graduates into the ASX 300. If large funds started buying or selling Lo-Cap shares, the resulting big price changes would make such shares too volatile for the fund managers.

The other important feature of large funds is that they do not cash out their holdings when a bear market appears. Instead they adjust the mix of shares that they hold so that their profit or loss stays as close as possible to the performance of the Australian All Ordinaries Index (XAO). So long as their results are no worse than the whole market result, they reason that they cannot be accused of mismanagement.

We small-fund (Lo-Cap) managers are not constrained by those rules, and so long as we strictly follow the rules that we teach, you can buy Lo-Cap shares that have greater profit potential. The bad news is that those shares are more volatile and therefore more risky to own. So we must stay smart, not commit too much of our kitty to any one of such shares, and monitor their price closely so we can sell any time their price violates our Stop-Loss price. Fortunately the brokerage fee for internet trading is small enough to justify selling and later buying back if a share price rebounds.

So more profit potential from higher risk Lo-Cap shares with future growth potential.

The tools we will use to trade such shares are position sizing to limit our exposure to any one company, and rising Stop-Loss prices to get us out quickly if the price plunges.

USING OUR TOOLS IS EASY

The strategies we use are not rocket science. We won't try to impress you by overcomplicating things or trying to reinvent global finance or say that everyone else is wrong and we're right. Each trading strategy has its benefits and you, as the trader, must educate yourself what these benefits are and how they apply to your situation.

If you can use, or can learn to use a computer, and particularly Microsoft Excel and are not frightened by simple arithmetic you should be quite comfortable using our tools.

To get the most out of our A-Line Trading Strategy having a personality that can organise your daily routine and methodically keep up with the simple chores that are involved is hugely beneficial. As you move towards retirement the importance of managing your investments becomes increasingly important, so you have a strong motive to exercise the self-discipline required.

OUR MANTRA:

If I can make a profit from share trading without losing those profits, then I will be able to live better for longer into my retirement, and won't have to rely on the government or relatives.

THE A-LINE TRADING STRATEGY

Discipline and self-motivation are the only essentials needed to be successful in trading.

The A-Line Trading Strategy is deceptively simple but we've worked on refining the following rules for a number of years to safeguard our own capital and manage risk in trading decisions before even considering sharing them. Follow these rules with rigor and well exercised self-discipline to maintain a reduced risk and increased potential of a better return on investment.

The A-Line Trading Strategy can be expressed in the following simple terms:

- Cut your losses but let your profits run.
- When a bull market stops rising, liquidate all shares and revert to cash in the bank.
- When a bear market stops falling and a bull market emerges start buying shares whose prices is rising.
- Use position sizing to spread your kitty across a number of shares held.
- When any share price falls too far you must sell it.
- Keep your eye on the ball; one half-hour each night is typical.
- Keep your emotions in check; think with your logic brain not your emotional brain.

Numerous traders emphasise that success lies more with your ability to sell than with which shares you buy. Many share-trading newsletters write mostly about buying, but our newsletter is written on the understanding that you will manage your self-managed share portfolio and that means taking responsibility to sell as well as buy at the appropriate times. You will be the one who decides that a share must be sold because its price has fallen below the Stop-Loss Price. We teach all new subscribers a simple tool to use which clearly charts the rising stop-loss price for you but unless you can find the time to use that tool each weekend, or preferably each evening, you are likely to get caught holding shares that should have been sold and encounter a loss.

You will notice that two key beliefs lie behind the A-Line Trading Strategy:

1. There is no such thing as a good share to buy and hold because all non-performing shares should be sold (in a major bear market nearly all shares fall together).

2. We traders cannot know the future direction the share market will take so the best we can do is to identify a price trend change when it happens and react accordingly. Fortunately our weekly newsletter will tell you the current trend of the XAO (Australian All Ordinaries Index) and also the current mood of investors (our A-Line index). From those two trends we will suggest an appropriate percentage of your share-trading kitty to hold in cash.

Each newsletter will contain a short lesson on using our simple trading tools to react to that data.

CAPITAL NEEDED TO START TRADING SHARES

One self-proclaimed trading guru is on record as saying that he won't assist anyone to trade shares who has less than $300,000 investment capital or who is not a bit smart. You need to ask your accountant and/or financial advisor if share trading is right for you and your situation as part of the due diligence we previously discussed in this document.

Buying and selling shares through an internet broker is much cheaper than using the old-style bricks-and mortar share brokerages but even so you need to ask Commsec, NabTrade or whoever your trading account is held with exactly what their charges will be. You will need to set up a bank account that is linked to your internet share trading platform so that you can transfer cash to and from it as required.

The other capital and then operating expense you cannot avoid is the purchase of a share charting package. We use a local package from Port Melbourne, Victoria called STEX Charting because it has special design features that suit the use of the A-Line Trading Strategy. STEX Investor Software also offer a program called STEX Portfolio Manager that runs alongside STEX Charting to track your portfolio's performance. Again you should make your own price enquiries from STEX Investor Software by calling (03) 9646 0109.

THE SHARE TRADING PROCESS

As set out in the previous section, the third rule of The A-Line Trading Strategy is to sell all shares at the start of a downwards bear market. New subscribers will be supplied with a manual that suggests how you can set out your buys and sells in a workbook, and then make the transactions over the internet.

We use an algorithm tuned to the Australian share market which accurately detects a change in investor mood before the market price-trend turns up or down.

We will not disclose the formula for that algorithm but in our weekly newsletter to subscribers we will report both the market price direction and the investor mood. Then based on that data we will advise the percentage of your kitty that we consider safe to have invested in shares at that stage.

Once the share market starts rising and we recommend spending some cash on buying rising shares, the two problems you have to solve are:

- Which shares should you buy and;
- How much money should spend on each different share.

Subscribers will find that we supply tools you can use in STEX Charting and in our Trader's Workbook software to solve these problems.

TRIALING THE A-LINE STRATEGY

Sign up for a subscription to The A-Line Newsletter though our website at:

www.aberdeentrading.com

You will receive:

- The weekly A-Line Newsletter.
-
- Our Subscriber's Manual along with our Trader's Workbook software for managing your trades.

You may decide to test the trading system and our tools by making paper trades, or to immediately set up to begin buying and selling shares. The latter approach will require you to acquire a share charting package and to register as a customer of an electronic share broker, with that service able to deposit and withdraw your funds from a nominated bank account.

IN CONCLUSION

Now that we have given you all this information it's up to you to digest it and apply what we have discussed to your situation and make a valued decision to either let us help you grow your wealth or not.

Please understand the following features of our service to you through our manuals and newsletters. Full Terms and Conditions can be found on our website.

We will not:

- Advise you on whether you should begin share trading: ask your accountant or financial advisor.
- Advise you on which shares to buy or sell because YOU will be the manager of your investments and we will not know, or indeed want to know, you financial situation.
- Discuss trading shares on overseas markets, nor trading such other financial instruments as futures, contracts, currencies, CFD's or other derivatives.
- Expect you to use our Trader's Workbook software efficiently until you have done a course or already possess good Microsoft Excel skills.

We will:

- Provide weekly advice on market price trend and investor mood.
- Inform you what percentage of your trading portfolio would be best held in shares and in cash at the present as suggested by the A-Line.

- Teach you how to use our Trader's Workbook software to determine position sizing and measure daily returns

on share investments from capital gains, dividends and bank interest.
- Inform you which of our tools you could use to identify shares to buy and what is our low-risk tool to signal when a share in your portfolio has passed the Stop-Loss price and should be sold immediately.
- Provide weekly results form a predefined hypothetical share trading portfolio, the Paper Portfolio, using our tools so that you can get the feel of the market when traded for low-risk results.
- Keep the newsletter brief and meaty so you can read it in two minutes without any waffle or sideshows.

APPENDICES

There is always more to learn. Here we provide you with more in-depth data to help your decision making process.

These appendices are here to provide you with more detailed information to aid in your decision making process and allow you to carry out your own due diligence prior to joining the A-Line Newsletter subscriber community.

CALCULATING COMPOUND INTEREST

The calculation of compound interest is often depicted as difficult mathematics, but in fact it is quite simple.

The relevance to self-managing share investments is that if you compare growth of several investments over time where both income earned and costs of operation differ you can discover surprising differences. The outcomes are as they say "counter-intuitive".

For that reason we have set out below a comparison of results after 20 years from three different investments:

- Interest earned from term loan deposits.
- Capital growth in a large managed fund.
- Growth from a self-managed fund.

The full workings are set out so that you can substitute what you believe or know to be the actual numbers in each working and can then compare them using a simple electronic calculator from the newsagent.

If you find such work beyond you, it is likely that you will also find managing a share portfolio yourself to be too difficult.

Working compound interest out on a calculator

First enter in the interest rate:

> e.g. 1.05 for 5% net P.A. return

Then the X sign then the starting capital

> e.g. $200,000

Then each press of the = sign shows the compound interest growth at 5% for another year.

Type of Investment	Interest Rate P.A.	20 Year Growth	Excess over term deposit	Excess %
Term deposit	4 %	$438,220	$0	0 %
Managed Fund	6 %	$641,420	$203,200	+46 %
Self-Managed Fund	9 %	$1,120,880	$682,660	+255%

Fig 1: Compound Interest over 20 years for $200,000 seed capital.

This should prove to you that you don't need a special financial calculator to construct a growth of compound interest table.

This type of calculation shows that earning a higher annual rate of return on your investment delivers a much higher retirement fund than the rate per annum suggests.

SELF-MANAGED SMALL SHARE FUNDS HAVE AN EDGE

There is a world of difference between managing share-trading in a multi-million dollar investment fund and self-managing your own small fund. The large fund deals mostly or exclusively with blue chip shares that own large amounts of capital (large-cap) and are included in the ASX300 group. It is not uncommon to see a share price jump once it graduates into the ASX 300. If large funds started buying or selling Lo-Cap shares, the resulting big price changes would make such shares too volatile for the fund managers.

The other important feature of large funds is that they do not cash out their holdings when a bear market appears. Instead they adjust the mix of shares that they hold so that their profit or loss stays as close as possible to the performance of the Australian All Ordinaries Index (XAO). So long as their results are no worse than the whole market result, they reason that they cannot be accused of mismanagement.

We small-fund (Lo-Cap) managers are not constrained by those rules, and so long as we strictly follow the rules that we teach, you can buy Lo-Cap shares that have greater profit potential. The bad news is that those shares are more volatile and therefore more risky to own. So we must stay smart, not commit too much of our kitty to any one of such shares, and monitor their price closely so we can sell any time their price violates our Stop-Loss price. Fortunately the brokerage fee for internet trading is small enough to justify selling and later buying back if a share price rebounds.

So more profit potential from higher risk Lo-Cap shares with future growth potential.

The tools we will use to trade such shares are position sizing to limit our exposure to any one company, and rising Stop-Loss prices to get us out quickly if the price plunges.

THANK YOU!

Thank you for reading our guide to Trading With The A-Line!

We hope what you have read has given you an insight into how accessible trading shares on the stock market is, what it takes to succeed and how you can apply our service to your own financial situation to help grown your net wealth.

If you're keen to find out more about The A-Line, how it works and how we apply it there is a lot more information available on our website. We also have a section dedicated to free resources to help you grow as a trader. We hope you enjoy them and find the resources useful.

Because this is only an introduction to sharer trading and trading using The A-Line Trading Strategy there is only a fraction of the information you need to know included in this book. We strongly recommend that you look at our suggested reading list on the website and, if you haven't already, start educating yourself in more depth.

Why share this information?

We had mentors early in our careers that showed us how to educate ourselves in the ways of the financial world. As they did for us, we do for you and this is our way of passing on the skills and lessons we have learned and along the way. Share trading is an interesting, extremely enjoyable and addictive game that can return very big rewards.

Happy investing!
The Aberdeen Trading Team

NOTES

www.ingramcontent.com/pod-product-compliance
Lightning Source LLC
Chambersburg PA
CBHW070434180526
45158CB00017B/1232